Hannah Linblater
31 Chester

The Giant Panda

The Giant Panda

Noel Simon

Translated and Adapted from texts by
Markus Kappeler and Jin Xuqi

Photographs by Jin Xuqi and others

可愛的大熊猫

J.M. Dent & Sons Ltd
London & Melbourne

This book arose through close collaboration with the Xinhua Publishing House in Beijing, China. We thank Xu Bang, the Editorial Director, and his colleagues for their attention to detail which has characterized this working partnership, and without which the project could not have succeeded. In particular we wish to express our appreciation to Jin Xuqi who not only took the photographs but also wrote the original text, and to Xu Peide who translated it from the Chinese.

This account incorporates the most up-to-date scientific information which Dr George B. Schaller, coordinator of the International Panda Conservation Programme, together with Chinese scientists, published in *The Giant Pandas of Wolong* (1985).

The Chinese characters on the title page mean 'The Lovely Giant Panda'.

Introducing the Giant Panda

The giant panda lives in China. In its native land it is known among other things as *daxiongmau*, which means 'large bear-cat'. This name is in fact somewhat misleading: the giant panda is certainly not a cat but is related to the bears. Yet although it looks like a bear it is not a very typical bear. It belongs neither to the family of the true bears – which includes both the black and brown bears and the polar bear – nor for that matter to the family of their smaller relatives, the raccoons, among which are the coati, the kinkajou and other species. Most scientists place the giant panda, together with its closest relative the lesser (or red) panda, in a separate panda family. This book will help you to find out about the natural history and habits of the giant panda and, in the process, you will come to appreciate why it is such a distinctive type of bear.

Very probably you will already have seen a panda in a zoo, or at least pictures of one. So you will know what this fascinating animal looks like: it is tubby and round-faced, with small erect ears and a black patch over each eye. Its black-and-white coat is, of course, both conspicuous and unusual. To understand why the giant panda has such strongly contrasting coloration you must realize two things. In the first place pandas are solitary animals; they prefer to be on their own. Secondly, although they have sensitive hearing and an acute sense of smell, their eyesight is not very good. Their colouring helps pandas to avoid encountering other pandas and thus unintentionally disturbing one another. Against the dense green vegetation of their natural habitat they can spot each other at a distance and so get out of each other's way. You might think that as they are so noticeable they will be more easily caught by predators. That could well happen if pandas were not extremely competent climbers. At the first sign of danger a panda climbs into the fork of the nearest tree, where it squats on its hindquarters without making a sound. High above the ground the black-and-white pattern of its coat acts as an effective camouflage: the black parts of the fur blend in with the dark trunk and branches, while the white parts become almost invisible against the bright sky. This reduces the animal's outline almost to vanishing point, and its enemy — whether leopard, brown bear, wild dog or human hunter — is unlikely to be able to see the panda properly even when standing directly below it. So its unusual markings mean that the panda can not only avoid unwanted meetings with other pandas but can also help reduce the chances of being spotted by enemies.

The giant panda's feeding habits are as unusual as its coloration. Although classified as a carnivore, or beast of prey, it differs from most other carnivores — the wolf, for example, or the tiger — by not eating meat. Neither is it omnivorous like its close relatives the true bears, who will eat virtually anything. The panda is a plant eater. Indeed, it confines itself to only a single group of plants: the bamboos. This explains why many people believe that it would be more logical to call it 'bamboo bear'. Now and again, of course, the panda nibbles at other plants. On rare occasions it may even happen that the clumsy creature accidentally swallows a careless bamboo rat, skin, hair and all. But normally it feeds exclusively on the stems, twigs, leaves and fresh young shoots of various types of bamboo, a diet that certainly has the merit of simplicity.

Bamboo, like grass — to which it is related — requires the animal eating it to have a specially equipped digestive system. The cow, for instance, which feeds on grass, has a stomach with four different compartments, and intestines that are forty to fifty meters in length. But the panda has an entirely different arrangement. It has the simple stomach of the carnivore with

The giant panda lives in China. At one time it was much more widespread, but today it is found in only a few isolated mountainous regions in the southwestern part of the country — places so remote and unspoiled that not a single road has yet cut through them. The panda's home lies among mountain ranges which rise tier upon tier in a series of gigantic steps to the Tibetan Plateau. The rugged peaks which crown these mountains are often hidden under thick cloud, and down their slopes thundering waterfalls plunge into deep valleys.

intestines that are barely ten meters long. It cannot therefore digest bamboo properly! And that fact naturally has important consequences: in order to extract enough nourishment from its food the panda has to consume an enormous quantity: ten to twenty kilograms a day. And in order to procure such a huge amount of plant material, it has to spend about fourteen hours a day feeding, day after day, summer and winter alike.

Almost two thirds of the panda's entire day is taken up with feeding. The little time that remains is mainly spent resting. It has no particular sleeping place but lies down on the ground wherever it happens to be. Whether it is day or night makes no difference whatever. When tired it simply flops on the ground for a few hours; when hungry it feeds for several hours at a stretch. Such is the panda's daily routine.

So few people have ever seen a panda in the wild state that it is not altogether surprising that various legends have built up around it. The local Tibetan people insist that the panda drinks water in such vast quantities that it sometimes becomes 'drunk'. One of the explanations given for this strange behaviour is that in early spring, when the warmer weather causes the snow to melt, pandas come down the mountain in search of water. The panda mistakes its own reflection in the water for another panda, and drinks as much as it can to prevent the other having it. Another version has it that the panda is so upset by the ceaseless babbling of the water that it tries to drink the stream dry once and for all! It is said to drink until it is hardly able to move. Collapsing on the ground, it remains in a stupor for several hours until it has slept off its 'drinking bout'. Tales of encounters with 'drunken' pandas abound . . . but, romantic as these stories are, there is not a shred of scientific evidence to support them.

In these remote mountains, covered with luxuriant forests of edible bamboo, the panda is at home. The bamboo is so dense that visibility is limited to a few meters. But the thick undergrowth is criss-crossed with tunnels through which the panda moves silently and quickly. Here it can move about freely, yet remain well concealed. The attractive, gentle creature in its black-and-white pelt in the picture on the left does not seem at all shy.

Pandas lead solitary lives. Wandering alone, each one gets to know every part of its own territory. Once a year males and females briefly pair off to breed.

A panda has no regular sleeping place. It simply lies on the ground; where and when is not important. In particularly bad weather it may shelter in a cave or a hollow tree like the one pictured below. Female pandas choose such places as dens in which to bear their young.

Pandas can live as long as thirty years, and attain a weight of about 120 kilograms. Full-grown pandas are about 1.5 meters tall when standing erect. Males and females are similar in appearance, except that females are slightly smaller. The two young pandas in this picture have still some way to grow. The panda's thick waterproof coat protects it from the cold and damp. The short, shaggy tail is normally hardly visible. Usually it lies concealed among the fur of the hindquarters. The tail protects the scent glands; it is also used as a brush to paint the animal's scent on to whatever it is marking. Powerful claws help this youngster to grip the tree.

The panda is seldom in a hurry: it ambles along at a leisurely pace with a rolling gait, paws turned inwards and head held low.

Normally the panda remains on the ground. But it is an extremely agile climber. Should danger threaten it will at once take refuge in a tree.

After a climbing expedition a little sleep is necessary, especially when the animal is as young as this one.

Pandas feed almost exclusively on bamboo. This plant – of which many different types are to be found in the mountain forests of China – is like a gigantic type of grass many meters high and with a stem the consistency of wood. Pandas like the juicy young bamboo shoots (pictured below). A panda consumes ten to twenty kilograms of bamboo every day. No wonder this one is as round as a barrel.

Hidden behind the panda's face are immense molars set in jaws activated by powerful chewing muscles. With these the animal can easily bite off and chew bamboo stalks. The panda's forepaws are very mobile and are specially adapted for grasping bamboo stalks: in the course of evolution it has developed a sixth digit on the forepaws. This so-called 'thumb', used in conjunction with the first 'finger', enables the panda to hold bamboo stems with great precision (as shown in the large photograph on the right). Eating tough cane can be hard work!

Pandas are related to bears and, like them, belong to the order of carnivores. Despite being a vegetarian, the panda at times relishes the taste of meat. But it is not itself a successful hunter and has little opportunity for helping itself to the kills of other animals. The best it can hope for is to catch some unsuspecting bamboo rat.

Although pandas feed almost entirely on bamboo, they now and again eat other plants. Even fruit, fungi and bark (opposite page, upper left) are occasionally included in their diet.

The tufted deer (opposite page, top right) is far too wary and alert ever to fall victim to the panda.

If, quite exceptionally, a panda ever preys on other animals, the evidence will later appear in its droppings. The droppings in the lower left-hand photograph contain hairs, while those on the right consist of nothing but undigested bamboo fibres.

23

Protecting the Giant Panda

You already know that the giant panda lives in China. China is a huge country – over thirty times larger than Great Britain. Within its habitat the panda is relatively numerous. Yet at the same time it is an extremely rare animal. Let me explain this apparent contradiction.

Giant pandas live in mist-shrouded forest at an altitude of between 1500 and 3500 meters. The vegetation is mainly bamboo which grows in dense thickets, giving the pandas the advantage of abundant food throughout the year. Here, too, are mountain streams and rivulets providing more than enough water to satisfy even the panda's enormous thirst. At these heights it is extremely cold, with frequent snow. But that doesn't worry the panda: its thick coat gives it good protection against both cold and damp.

Centuries ago forests similar to those in which the panda lives were widespread in China. In those days there were comparatively few people in that vast country. But as the number of people steadily increased they cleared the forests to make way for villages and rice fields, using the timber to build houses and as fuel for cooking and heating. So, bit by bit, the panda's habitat shrank. What is more, people hunted the black-and-white animal, for panda skins were popular as sleeping mats. Besides being soft and warm, they were believed to ward off evil spirits. Pandas were therefore forced to retreat ever deeper into the mountains.

Today giant pandas are found in only a few remote mountain regions in southwestern China: in the Qionglai, the Daxiangling, the Xiaoxiongling and Liang Mountains (Sichuan Province), the Min Mountains (Sichwan Gansu Provinces), as well as in the Qinling Range (Shaanxi Province).

At most there are one thousand of these 'national treasures' – as pandas are officially designated – in China today. That is not really very many. Indeed, the giant panda is regarded as one of the world's rarest animals.

The important question is whether the giant panda is likely to become extinct in the near future. Unfortunately it is impossible to give a simple answer. All that can be said with certainty is that the survival of the last remaining pandas cannot be taken for granted, but that everything humanly possible is being done to safeguard them.

For a number of years the giant panda has been strictly protected by the government of China. Hunting is totally prohibited and carries severe penalties. Twelve panda sanctuaries, or reserves, have already been established to protect large stretches of suitable habitat and to provide living space for up to 500 or 600 pandas. An important factor is the affection in which the panda is nowadays held by the Chinese people. The panda can be seen as a symbol of China's determination to treat the conservation of the country's wildlife and natural resources with the seriousness it deserves.

A few years ago there was a set-back which, as it occurs only once or twice a century, nobody had accurately foreseen: the bamboo in several of the sanctuaries began to flower. Whole thickets of bamboo came into bloom, looking absolutely lovely. But for the pandas the sight was far from pleasing. Once bamboos have blossomed and formed seed, they wither and die. That is a perfectly normal part of this plant's life cycle, and happens every few decades. Sometimes the die-back is spread over a number of years. For pandas living in an affected area it results in a lengthy famine which lasts until the seed has germinated and young bamboo shoots have reappeared.

In the past it was easier for the pandas to survive such a catastrophe. If the bamboo in one forest died back the animals could simply move to another where food was still plentiful, either from one mountain range to another or from the upper parts of the mountains down into the valleys. But today the pandas are confined to their last strongholds; hemmed in by human settlements and cultivated land, they have nowhere else to go. During the last few years about two hundred are known to have died from starvation. As long as the threat of bamboo die-

The following page shows a snow-covered mountainside in the Wolong Reserve. With a surface area of 2000 square kilometers, it is the largest of the twelve special panda reserves. Wolong has a population of more than 100 pandas. Early in 1984 – a bitterly cold winter – an unusual event occurred which you can see in the sequence of pictures on pages 28 to 34.

back exists there must be at least some uncertainty over the future of the last remaining pandas.

But there is no need to be too depressed as the people of China have no intention of leaving their favourite animal in the lurch. In the worst-hit areas the local peasants have established feeding places where, day after day, large bales of food are put out for the pandas. Rescue teams comb the forests searching for weak or sick animals. Any they find are brought in to a reception camp. There they are cared for by specialists. After being restored to health, they are taken to another area containing healthy stands of bamboo and released. Volunteers help to counter future famines by planting large areas with bamboo.

A comprehensive conservation programme has already been started, with a team of Chinese and American scientists working in the reserves studying the panda, about which many details are still unknown. The more the animal's natural history is understood the better the prospects of helping it. Only if everything is properly organized will the giant panda be able to overcome the difficulties facing its survival in the wild state.

Tremendous efforts are also being taken in China to breed pandas in captivity. There are currently about seventy giant pandas in Chinese zoological gardens. They are the zoos' biggest attractions and their enclosures are invariably surrounded by enthusiastic visitors. More than forty pandas have already been distributed to zoos all over the world. But the scientists know that a great deal remains to be done, and are constantly searching for means of improving breeding results. Artificial insemination is one of the techniques they are trying to perfect. This is necessary because pandas seldom mate in captivity. But, by using artificial insemination, a female panda can conceive and bear young without having to mate. The breeding programme is being developed in the hope that one day it will be sufficiently successful to enable suitable parts of the panda's natural habitat to be re-stocked with animals born and raised in zoos.

During the summer of 1983 large areas of bamboo came into flower in various parts of the reserve. The following winter entire colonies of bamboo withered and died. Pandas living in the reserve had a hard time. There was little for them to eat. Among the starving pandas was an old female. Where among this devastation could she find something to eat? As she searched desperately for food, a delicious smell suddenly came to her nostrils. Where on earth could it have come from?

Hesitating only for a moment she followed the scent. At every step she sank into soft snow. Here you can see her track. Suddenly she came across a curious shelter which was, in fact, a trap for catching pandas. Nearby, a man was warming himself by a fire. Quite by chance, the shy female panda had stumbled across the camp of a panda rescue team. Hunger soon overcame her fears. She even grabbed a stick of juicy sugar cane, and evidently found it just as delicious as bamboo.

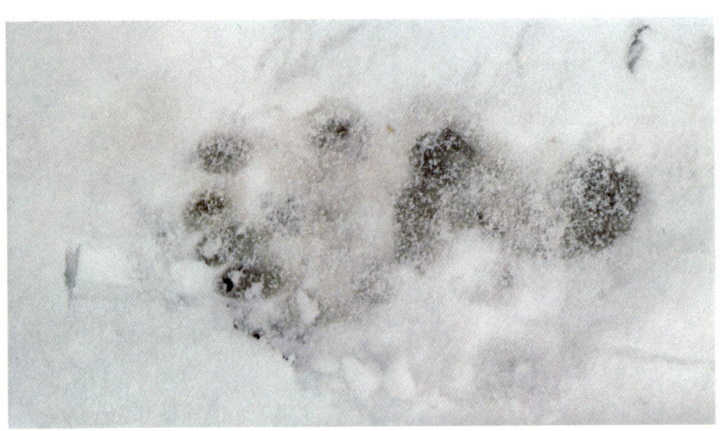

The people from the rescue party were delighted with their guest. She was the tamest and most trusting panda they had ever met. Usually starving animals had first to be trapped and then — as in the picture on the left — carried on a fatiguing foot-

march down the mountain before being released into a holding pen at the reception camp. There the pandas could be held and fed until they were fit again.

But this particular female simply took up residence in the vicinity of the reception camp. She did not require any help. She knew when she was well off, and how to look after herself. She found the delicious smell from the kitchen and the cook's tent almost irresistible. Roast mutton was something new in her experience, and tasted absolutely delectable!

Birth and Upbringing

In the holding pen the starving pandas are fed nourishing rice gruel. Pandas quickly acquire a taste for it. The youngster on the left did not take long to learn to eat an entire dish.

Our female panda remained more than a month in the vicinity of the reception camp and was always tame and friendly. Every day she took the food which had been prepared for her. When her weight eventually increased from 67 to 90 kilograms she was taken many kilometers away and released in an area where there was plenty of bamboo: from then on she could fend for herself again.

There is one great disadvantage in eating bamboo: the giant panda has to spend so much time satisfying its hunger. On the other hand, a bamboo diet also has certain advantages. To start with, practically no other animal competes with the panda for its food. Secondly, bamboo is available in abundance at all seasons of the year, even in winter. The panda is not therefore forced to hibernate in winter through shortage of food like, for instance, the polar bear. Neither is it necessary for it to lay down a stock of winter food like the squirrel, or to migrate southwards in winter like the stork. It can remain in its habitat throughout the year and always be sure of finding enough to eat – as long as the bamboo does not come into flower. A typical panda territory is about two to three kilometers in diameter. Normally the panda spends its whole life there. But it does not keep its territory entirely to itself, as many other animals do. It is not in the least put out if other pandas move in – as long as any new arrival does not come too close. The panda prefers to be alone.

From time to time pandas naturally mate and have young. For this it is obviously necessary that males and females should occasionally meet. How do these unsociable animals, who normally go out of their way to avoid others of their own kind, manage to find one another? How can animals that are ready to mate know where to find a suitable partner?

Pandas, like many other animals, have solved this difficulty in a simple but effective way. They 'notify' one another by scent marking. From time to time during the course of its foraging expeditions the panda will pause in its feeding to rub its hindquarters – where there are special scent glands – against a tree trunk, stump or rock, leaving a series of scented messages for other pandas. These distinctive messages are a way of announcing either that the animal concerned is not far away and wants to be left in peace, or that it wishes to have young and is looking for a mate. In this way males and females inform each other of their whereabouts and whether they are ready to mate or not. This 'information service', based on scent marking, functions not only at mating time and between males and females but between all pandas at all times.

The mating instinct is strongest in the spring when the days start to lengthen, the trees come into fresh leaf and the birds burst into song. A male panda coming across the scent marks left by a female ready to mate follows the alluring trail. But he is careful to avoid approaching the female too closely, as at first this will put her off. Unless the male can curb his impatience the female is likely to cuff him with her sharply clawed paws, or bite him. She needs time in which to become accustomed to the strange male – for females generally have a different partner each year. The male may have to wait a long time before the female accepts him. Sometimes he shows his feelings by climbing a tree and giving a series of muffled barks and roars. At the same time he tries to impress the female with what a bold and resourceful creature he really is. His roars are intended partly for that purpose and partly to warn off other males who may be inclined to appear and perhaps disrupt the mating. Several days may be needed before the female is willing to accept the male. His patience is eventually rewarded and he is allowed to approach and mate with her. When mating, the female normally crouches on the ground in front of the male with her muzzle tucked in to her chest and her forepaws covering her eyes. The male squats behind her and leans upon her with his forepaws on the lower part of her back. He then mounts her and completes the mating. A short while later the two animals part and go their separate ways. The male has no fatherly feelings at all towards his offspring.

In autumn, after a gestation period of five months, and in the safety of a cave or hollow tree, the female gives birth. Sometimes she has twins, but the second cub seldom survives.

The newborn panda is absolutely minute: it weighs about 100 grams and is only 15 centimeters long – barely as large as a golden hamster. The tiny cub cannot at first open its eyes and is

Spring, the mating season, is an exciting time of the year for pandas.

The males are overcome by the seductive scents of the females and compulsively follow their tracks. But a female does not submit to a male until she has first accustomed herself to her prospective partner.

In the upper picture a female has fled up a tree to escape the attentions of an impatient male (below). The male gazes up at her, hoping that she will soon come down and allow him to mate.

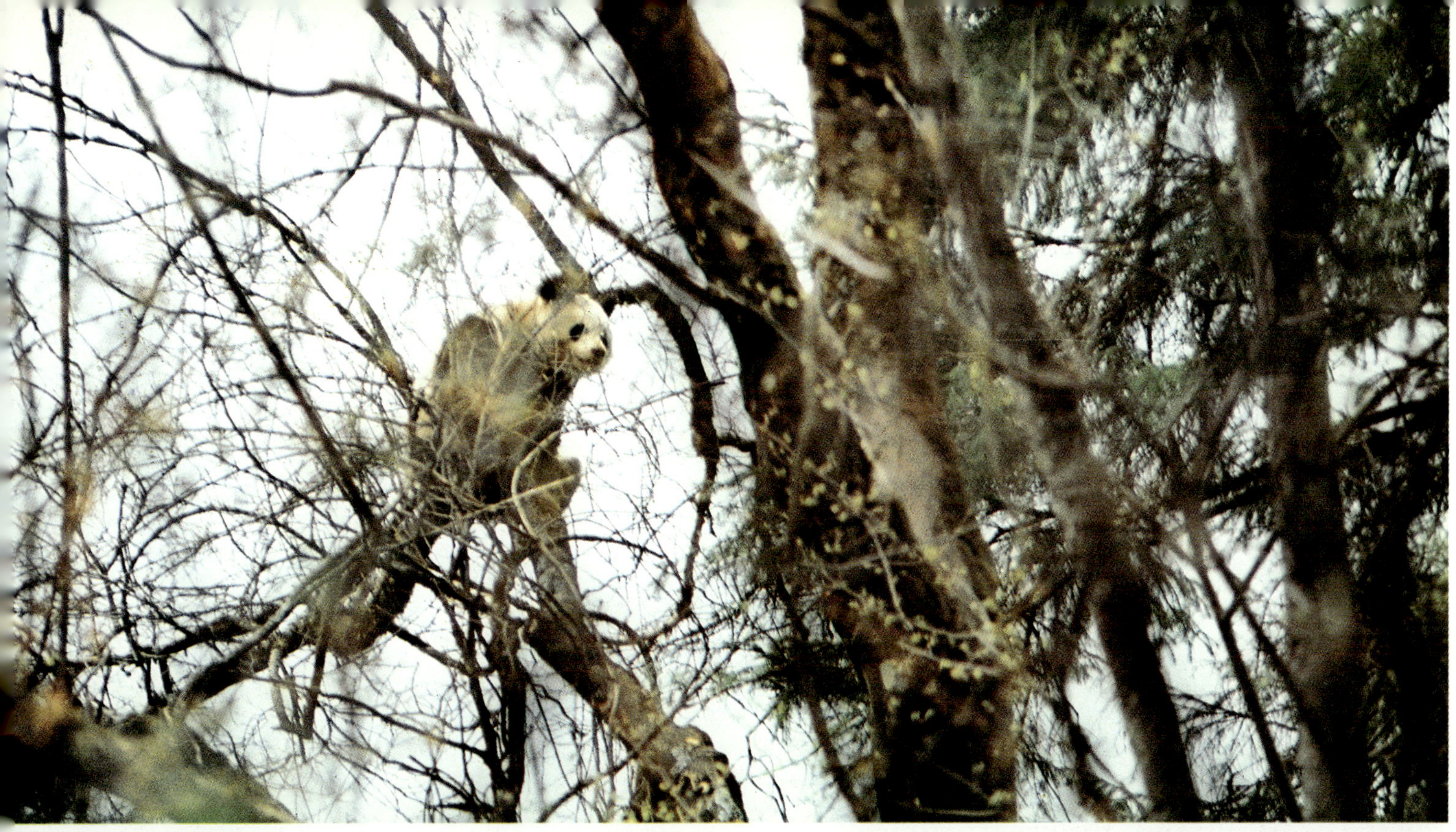

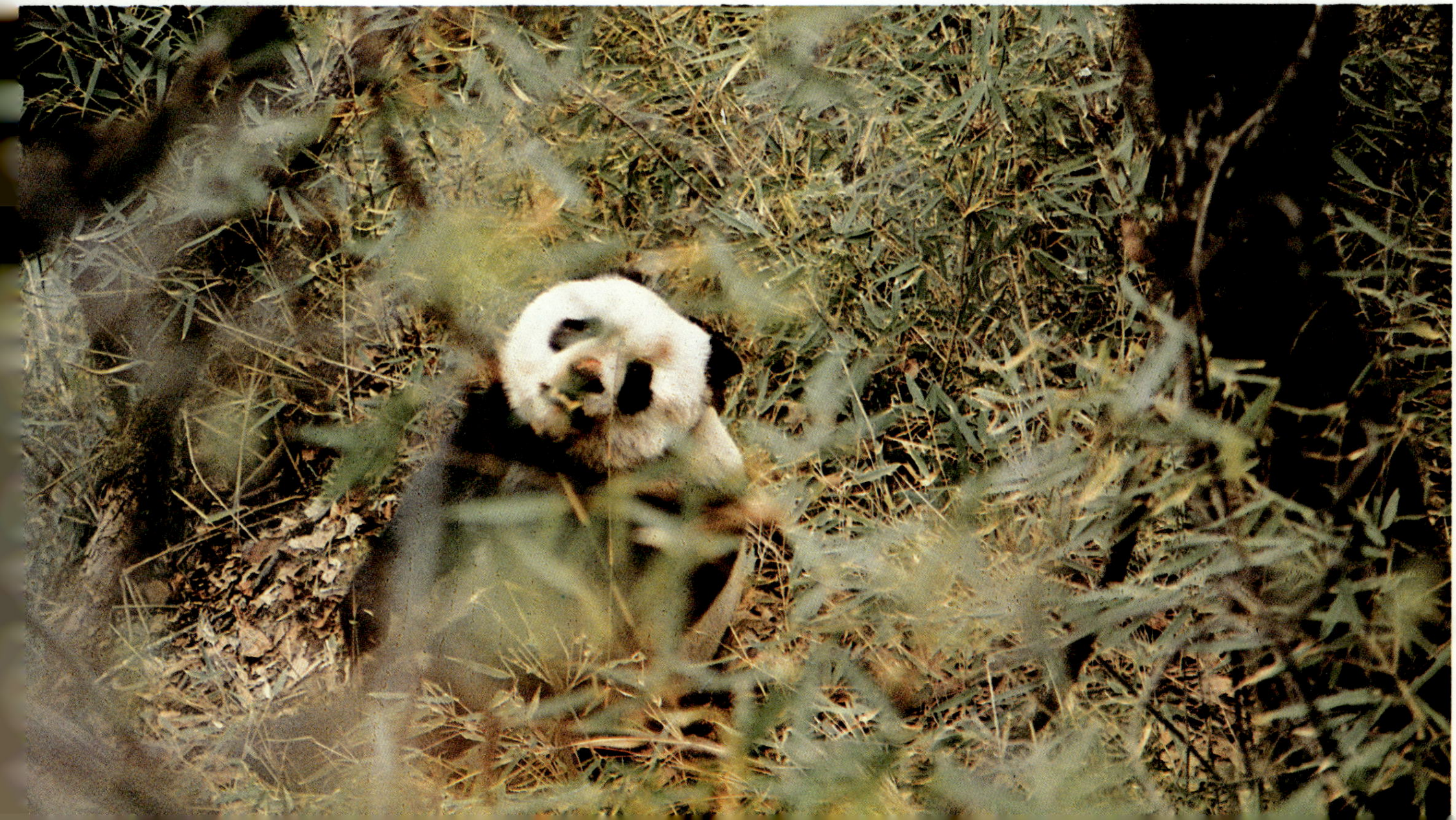

utterly helpless. It is practically naked, its pale skin being covered with a fine down of fluffy hairs. Nor does it have teeth. The female panda is a conscientious mother and devotes herself to her offspring. For the first few weeks of its life she holds her cub in her arms, never for an instant letting it go. Cradled in her arms it is totally protected from wind and weather as well as from enemies. She holds it tenderly against her breast while it suckles, and constantly licks it to keep it thoroughly clean. The habit of carrying her young in her arms may be one of the reasons why a female panda normally raises only one cub: she would have difficulty in holding two.

Under its mother's solicitous care the young cub grows rapidly. Its sparse covering of hair gradually thickens, and before long it is possible to make out the characteristic coat colouring: the black eye patches appear on about the sixth day, followed by the ear and shoulder markings; last of all the fore- and hind-legs. After about one month the cub opens its eyes and stares at its surroundings. At this stage it weighs one kilogram. At three months the cub can crawl about on its own, and its first teeth are already through. By the time it is four months of age it can move about quite rapidly.

In the following months the panda cub must learn from its mother all the things that it needs to know so that it can cope as an adult. For example, when danger threatens it must immediately climb the nearest tree and conceal itself in the branches. It must know where to find juicy young bamboo shoots and learn how to bite them off; to drink from a stream without falling in; how and where to leave its scent – and many other important matters. Eventually, at the age of about one and a half years, the cub is sufficiently self-reliant to start leading an independent life. Leaving its mother, it goes in search of a suitable territory of its own. There it settles down with only itself to think about. And when in due course the young panda reaches the age of five to seven years it can set about looking for a mate and starting a family of its own.

The mating season is the only time of the year when the normally solitary pandas come briefly together. During the mating (pictured left) the male releases his semen into the female, thus enabling her to conceive.

On a number of occasions pandas have successfully reproduced in captivity. The female on the right is called Mei-Mei. She holds her newborn first son, Ron-Shun, tenderly in her arms. The tiny rose-pink creature weighs only 100 grams. These two pandas live in the Chengdu Zoo in China.

Ron-Shun, now seventeen days old, has a very loud voice. Normally Mei-Mei carries him in her arms. If, even for a moment, she puts him down, as in the accompanying picture, he screams with indignation at the top of his voice. Mei-Mei at once tries to comfort her noisy little offspring.

See how contentedly mother and son lie here. Ron-Shun is now four weeks old and weighs about one kilogram. He is no longer rose-coloured as he was at birth. His coat has thickened out and become black-and-white in colour. Already he is recognizable as a panda. In another fortnight he will begin to crawl.

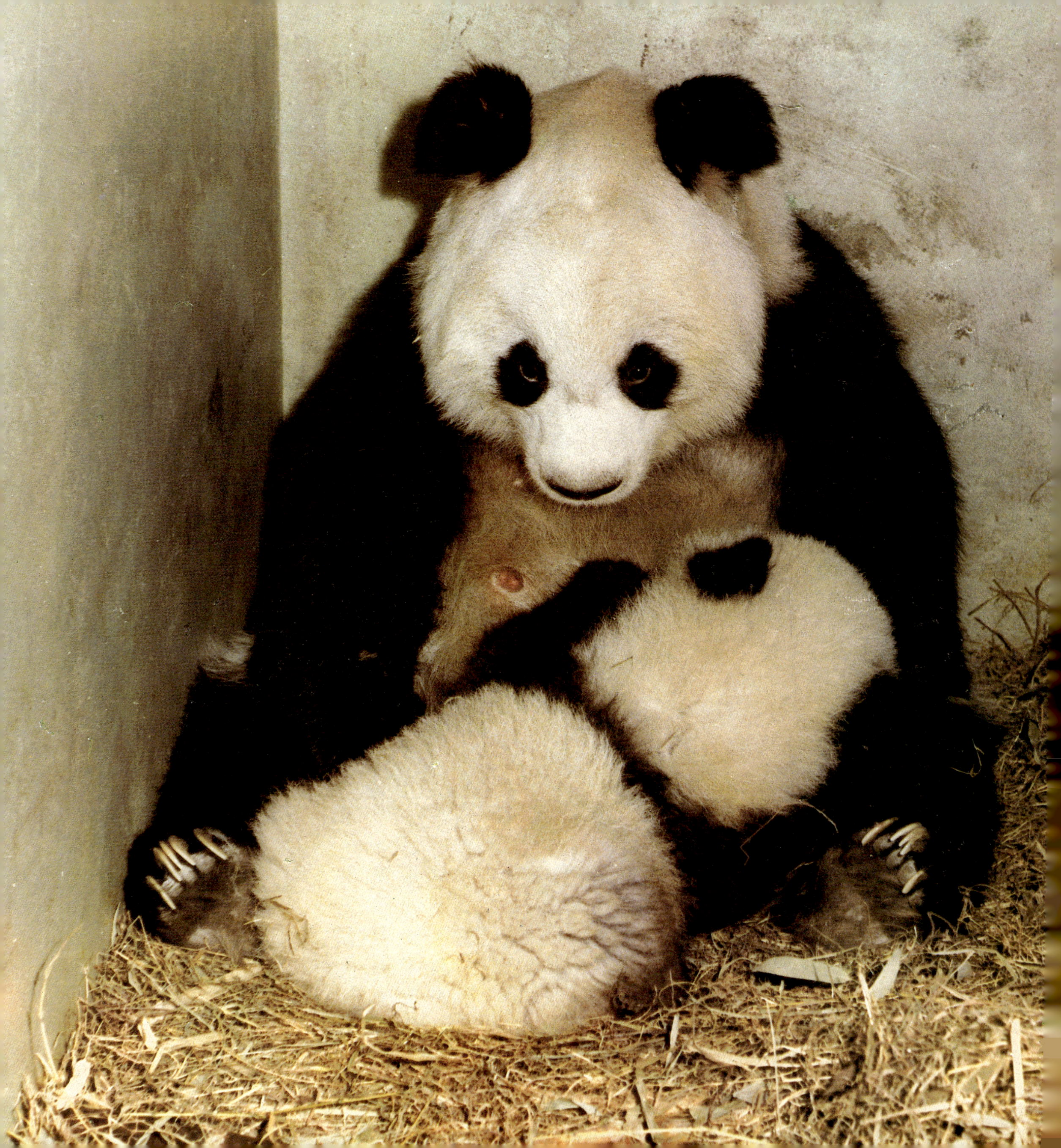

Ron-Shun is now five months old and weighs ten kilograms. Mei-Mei is no longer able to carry him constantly in her arms. He must therefore either lie or sit on the ground in order to suckle. As he drinks, his mother repeatedly and lovingly licks his muzzle clean.

Ron-Shun took his first unsteady steps when he was not quite three months old. Now, two months later, he can already move about like an adult, without constantly stumbling and falling on his nose.

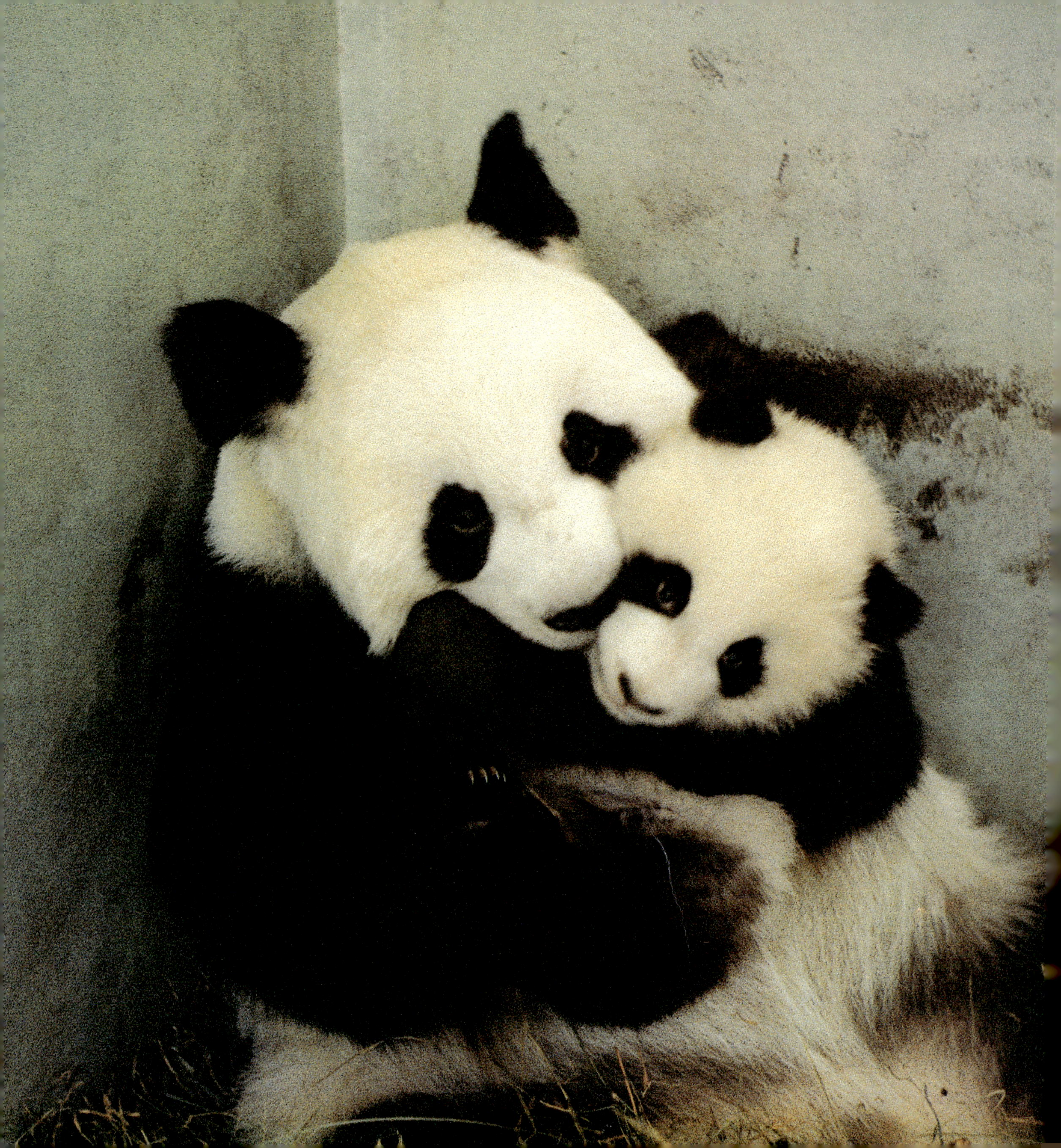

Ron-Shun loves all kinds of games. One of his favourite is to clamber on his mother's back and slither down her side. Sometimes he is so high-spirited that he turns a series of somersaults. Mei-Mei adores her lively son and loves cuddling him.

Here is Ron-Shun at the age of one year and weighing about 30 kilograms. He has given up suckling Mei-Mei and taken to chewing bamboo. He likes to roam around his enclosure at the zoo; there is always something new to discover.

If Ron-Shun were living in the wild he would soon have to leave his mother and establish his own territory. The first weeks of independence can be a difficult time for the young panda: thrown on his own resources, he has to put into practice all the lessons he has learned from his mother.

Jin Xuqi spent many years with her camera trailing the giant panda through the bamboo forests of China. The black-and-white panda is a very rare animal: only about one thousand survive in remote and widely separated parts of that vast country. Jin Xuqi was fortunate to have been able to take these superb photographs. How this fascinating animal lives and why it is endangered is told by Markus Kappeler. The text has been translated and adapted by Noel Simon who, as compiler of the original *Mammalia* volume of the *Red Data Book* – published by the International Union for Conservation of Nature and Natural Resources (IUCN) – was responsible for placing the giant panda on the official list of the world's rare and endangered species.

Picture Credits

Jin Xuqi: Page 4 (outer left and right), 7, 10, 11, 13, 14, 15, 16 (upper and lower), 17, 18, 20/21, 22, 23 (lower right), 26/27, 32 (left and right), 39, 40, 41, 42, 43, 44, 46, 47

Chen Jie: Page 2, 4 (third picture from left), 9, 21 (lower), 30 (lower right), 34

Deng Qitao: 20, 23 (upper right), 30 (top), 37 (top and bottom)

Hu Jinchu: 17, 21 (top), 23 (lower left), 30 (lower left), 38

Meng Qingbao: 45

Pan Wenshi: 12, 19 (left), 23 (upper left and centre)

Pu Tao: 19 (right)

Shi Junyi: 4 (second picture from left), 28, 29, 31, 33 (all)

Alain Rainon/Jacana: cover picture

First published in Great Britain 1986
English translation © J.M. Dent & Sons Ltd
Originally published in German under the title
Der Grosse Panda
© Kinderbuchverlag KBV Luzern AG 1986
All rights reserved

Printed in Italy
This book is set in 14/16½ Linotron Century Schoolbook
by Tradespools Limited, Frome, Somerset

British Library Cataloguing in Publication Data

Simon, Noel
  The giant panda.
  1. Giant panda—Juvenile literature
  I. Title   II. Xuqi, Jin
  599.74'443   QL737.C214

ISBN 0-460-06249-2